I0469474

mike kresch

WINNING THE
MVB
(MOST VALUABLE BRAND)

*Insight, Strategy, and Tactics from a
Passionate Personal Branding Strategist*

Copyright © 2015 Mike Kresch.

All rights reserved. No part of this book may be reproduced, stored, or transmitted by any means—whether auditory, graphic, mechanical, or electronic—without written permission of both publisher and author, except in the case of brief excerpts used in critical articles and reviews. Unauthorized reproduction of any part of this work is illegal and is punishable by law.

ISBN: 978-1-4834-3127-7 (sc)
ISBN: 978-1-4834-3126-0 (e)

Because of the dynamic nature of the Internet, any web addresses or links contained in this book may have changed since publication and may no longer be valid. The views expressed in this work are solely those of the author and do not necessarily reflect the views of the publisher, and the publisher hereby disclaims any responsibility for them.

Any people depicted in stock imagery provided by Thinkstock are models, and such images are being used for illustrative purposes only. Certain stock imagery © Thinkstock.

Lulu Publishing Services rev. date: 05/26/2015

Dedication

For Steph, Sam, and Ruby.
I love you more than words can say.

Contents

Introduction

• • •

What is Personal Branding?

This is probably a question many of you might have before we even get started. Here's the short answer: personal branding takes marketing insight, strategy, and tactics that, until recently, have been reserved for businesses and applies them to individuals to help them create value and opportunity in their careers and lives.

Let me elaborate on this for you with concrete examples. Most successful brands, such as Geico, Subway, and Cadillac, go through significant strategic planning periods for their brands. This process often includes multiple ad agencies and countless hours of hard work. The strong marketing we see in the form of advertising, direct mail, and social media is an offshoot of this. When done right, growth and market share increases are a logical conclusion to the process.

People, on the other hand, often behave in the exact opposite fashion. They fly by the seat of their pants and tend to be reactive to circumstance and environment. They make impromptu resolutions at random moments. They decide to look for new jobs when they hit their lowest point. There is very little proactivity or formal strategic thought with regard to personal brands, and results tend to reflect this. Yet, often, people are shocked when they don't see the growth and opportunity they had hoped for. To help put people on a more targeted path to success, personal branding introduces and applies a new, structured level of proactive strategic planning and thought.

Here's a more tactical example: Businesses realize that in today's world, when an Internet search using Google, Yahoo, or Bing, is done in their category, if they don't rank high enough, their chances of winning the business decrease substantially. Accordingly, they allocate a percentage of their marketing budget to search engine optimization (SEO) and search engine marketing (SEM) to help them consistently rank higher.

People also need to realize that every day, others are searching for them, or people like them, on LinkedIn and on the Web. How people rank in searches can have a huge impact on their professional careers. And when searches do take place, what results do others see? Search results need to yield strong content that makes brands stand out and shine. Personal branding helps people optimize both their social/digital presence and personal SEO, so when others conduct searches for them, they find them easily and come away impressed.

Don't get me wrong; I am not saying that individuals have to imitate big businesses in everything they do to lead more successful careers and lives. Much of the material in this book has zero correlation to any corporate marketing behavior or protocol. I do, however, see tremendous opportunity for growth by imitating some of the marketing habits and thought processes that have made corporate brands incredibly successful.

In general, people need to change their mindsets, and begin to treat themselves as brands that exist in an extremely competitive environment. I am firmly convinced that, moving forward, personal branding is going to be a huge factor in the professional realm. People who devote the proper amount of time, energy, and creativity to their personal brands are going to be the ones who stand out, cut through the clutter, and reach MVB (Most Valuable Brand) status. This will pay tremendous dividends, both short term and long term.

Chapter 1

● ● ●

Attaining MVB Status

In professional sports leagues, the most prestigious individual award an athlete can win is the Most Valuable Player (MVP). This designation is usually restricted to one or two people per season. Unlike sports, the Most Valuable Brand (MVB) status is not restricted to an elite few—every one of us can attain it!

How does one identify MVB winners? Here are ten characteristics, in no particular order, which they exhibit:

(1) They have a growth strategy for their brand in place. They are not just winging it or going through the motions. They have a mission with short and long-term objectives. MVBs take a strategic approach.

(2) They are authentic and always stay "on brand." No matter what happens, MVBs remain true to themselves. They celebrate their individuality and consistently bring their strongest brand attributes to the forefront.

(3) *They are happy at work.* This doesn't mean they never have a bad day—everyone does. On the whole, they like going to work, enjoy the company of those around them, feel comfortable with their level of responsibility, and are compensated properly.

(4) *They rank well in a search.* Whether it's LinkedIn, Google, Yahoo, or Bing, when you enter an MVB's name in any search, you're not going to have difficulty tracking her/him down, because they're going to pop up frequently. And no matter where you click to get more information, your first impression is going to be a good one.

(5) *They have a strong social media presence.* When you visit any MVB's social presence, you come away with a clear picture of who they are and what they stand for. They say and do the right things and stay in contact with their followers appropriately.

(6) *They learn new skills.* Never the type to be complacent, MVBs are constantly learning new skills, taking courses, and garnering certifications. It's not just for show; they apply the newfound knowledge whenever possible to bolster their performance.

(7) *They have a valuable, growing network of contacts, followers, and friends.* MVBs have significant professional networks. They have high-level contacts who know, understand, appreciate, and engage with their brands. The number of quality contacts grows consistently over time.

(8) *They give back.* MVBs give back in many ways; they are active in the local community, with their former alma maters, and/or with charitable organizations. They are the first people to support causes when they can and participate because it's the right thing to do. They also garner significant respect in the process.

(9) They try new things without trepidation. MVBs relish new opportunities to grow value and create opportunities for themselves. They follow trends in marketing and technology and are not afraid to be at the forefront of something new, even if it means being the first among their peer group to try something out.

(10) They are prepared for anything. If a huge new job or other professional opportunity suddenly presents itself, MVBs are ready to pounce on it without hesitation. On the flip side, if a sudden, unexpected turn for the worse takes place on the job front, it's just a blip on the radar for them. They are fully prepared to move onto the next opportunity and have all the resources in place to get them there quickly.

MVBs are the rock stars of the professional world. And they reap the benefits of this status. My own mission is simple: to help all of you attain this status.

Chapter 2

● ● ◉ ◦

My Story

For the purpose of this book, my story starts on a cold evening in January 2012—one of the best nights of my life. I was honored with a major award at my former company, which was handed out to only the top 1 percent of the past year's performers. Along with about fifty other employees, I was honored at a beautiful ceremony on the forty-fourth floor of our building in midtown Manhattan. My boss made a beautiful speech (you can read a transcript on my LinkedIn profile), and my wife Stephanie was invited to be on hand, which meant the world to me. I was given a spot bonus and told that I was a major part of the company's future. After the ceremony, I was given carte blanche: "Take Stephanie out for dinner, anywhere you like, on us." In retrospect, I wish I had taken her to Nobu or Jean Georges instead of the neighborhood sushi joint.

I can look back on this night and objectively say that it had an incredibly positive effect on me. The honor didn't go to my head, and I was motivated as hell to prove that the designation was no fluke. I wanted to win it again, worked my ass off, and did some of the best work of my life in the next year and a half.

Fast-forward to Wednesday June 5, 2013 at 3:00 P.M. I answered the phone in my office to find my friend from human resources on the other line.

"Mike, it's Mary. Do you mind coming down to my office for a moment?"

"Sure," I responded, suddenly aware that my life was about to change dramatically.

I was promptly let go, after twelve years, from a company and a job that I loved. I felt only days removed from the glory of winning my award.

The story behind being let go isn't important at this point. Was it unfair? Hell yes, but as I teach my kids: life isn't fair, and once you accept that fact, it gets a little bit easier to deal with the nonsense that sets you back. The important thing is, in the immortal words of Rocky Balboa, *"It's about how hard you can get hit and keep moving forward."* Amen, Rock.

I suddenly found myself with time for introspection. I was an accomplished, award-winning marketing executive, but my career had been established in publishing, where most management careers weren't taking off anymore. If anything, most people in my position were entrenched in battles to maintain their current positions. That's not good. I had a series of meetings over the next few months that reconfirmed my own preliminary assessment: To stay in the industry, unless I was really lucky, I would have to take a pay cut and probably never rise to the level I had achieved. This wasn't acceptable to me. So it was on to bigger and better things.

The million-dollar question is "What?" I was very confident in my ability as a marketer to help businesses grow, so this seemed to be a logical starting point. I jumped right in and started my own company without a business plan—you can judge for yourself whether that was a bad idea or not. I think it probably was. But in any event, I adapted on the fly. I knew from the onset that sooner, rather than later, it would behoove me to find a niche and, in doing so, make sure it was something that I firmly believed in.

Before long, I found my niche. I've always been passionate about personal branding and paid careful attention to it throughout my career. It's a natural inclination for marketers. More importantly, I see a strong demand for help in this realm. My new mission is to leverage my experience, marketing expertise, and (most importantly) passion for helping others to help professionals thrive in this crazy economy that we're immersed in today.

Chapter 3

● ● ●

SWOT Analysis

Most well-established businesses start their year with a strategic marketing plan. Levels of detail, effort, and sophistication that go into these plans vary by company size, positioning, strategic objectives, stage of growth, and other relevant factors.

Then, there's us people. Instead of crafting marketing plans for our own brands, most of us make a bunch of half-baked New Year's resolutions that are not thought out well and usually fall by the wayside, often becoming a distant memory by the first signs of spring.

Making your personal brand stand out means treating it more like a well-run business. It should start with smart, strategic planning, and continue with effective tactical implementation. Here's the beauty of it: It doesn't matter where you currently stand in your professional life, and it doesn't matter what time of year it is. You can start growing your personal brand strategically today, and it can be fun.

One way to start is with a classic marketing exercise: a SWOT analysis of your brand. SWOT is an acronym for **strengths, weaknesses, opportunities, and threats**. I've been a part of many SWOT analysis sessions, and I find them to be quite effective as a preliminary step in crafting a strategy. In the corporate world, here's how it typically goes: a group of people gets together and sits around a white board. A brainstorming session takes place, resulting in the collection of a lot of strong, raw, and honest information. The results are added to the overall mix of data used to form an annual strategic plan.

The same basic rules apply to personal branding, with a few subtle differences and approaches.

Creating Your Own Personal Board of Directors

You're ready to start working on your personal brand, and it starts with a SWOT analysis. Whom do you get to work with you? Answer: you create your own informal board of directors to help. I recommend three people who you are very close to, outside the realm of immediate family and significant others/ partners. Pick three of your smartest, most well-rounded friends or coworkers. Ideally it's a mix of people from different walks of life, backgrounds, etc. Their common interest needs to be you; they need to care deeply and not be afraid to speak the truth.

You will need about an hour and a half of their time—a nice gesture is to have them over to your home/apartment and treat them to a meal. The session itself should take an hour with consecutive fifteen minute brainstorming intervals devoted to each of the four categories: strengths, weaknesses, opportunities, and strengths.

To better illustrate the concept, let's take a look at a fictitious person named Sam, a 35-year-old law associate who aspires to become a partner at his firm. Happily married and a father of two young boys, ages six and three, Sam wants to do everything within his power to cultivate his personal brand in a way that separates himself from other associates who are also vying for a few coveted partnership spots. In starting the SWOT process, he has selected his team of three to serve as his board of directors: his college roommate, a friend from law school, and his current assistant at the firm. They get together and proceed to do a great job on the analysis.

Some of the raw data from their hour-long session includes:

Strengths:

- *Sam has a great personality—a true "people person" who people gravitate toward.*
- *Strong organizational skills: "One of the most buttoned-up people I know."*
- *Incredible expertise!*
- *Always punctual, sharply dressed, etc. Carries himself like a partner.*

Weaknesses:

- *Not always as assertive in situations where he needs to be.*
- *Not active in social media.*
- *Not generating enough new business for the firm.*
- *Not involved in the community, mostly due to a lack of time.*

Opportunities:

- *Showcase expertise by blogging and creating content.*
- *More networking to generate new business for the firm.*
- *More active on social networks to show the well-rounded nature of his personality.*

- *Coaching his kid's sports teams is a way to spend more time with family and become more active within the community.*

Threats:

- *Other more aggressive associates without families have more time to devote to their career and might be on a faster track to partnership.*
- *The firm may not be growing fast enough to offer the right amount of partnership opportunities.*

As a starting point, we've given Sam a lot to think about as he approaches the upcoming year. He now has his own personal board of directors that has become actively engaged in his efforts to grow his personal brand.

However, we might still need more data before formally crafting a smart, viable strategy. We have collected valuable insight from three people within Sam's inner circle. But what do his clients think his strengths are? How about his immediate boss or other partners within the firm? We can "extend out" and collect great data from a broader group through one of the most valuable tools in the personal branding space: a 360Reach Brand Survey.

Chapter 4

• • •

360REACH Brand Survey

As soon as I decided to transition into the personal branding space, I took a deep dive into online research on the topic. In a fragmented market, one name consistently climbed to the forefront: William Arruda, the founder of Reach Personal Branding. William is a former IBM marketer and a visionary who is often referred to as one of the "founding fathers" of personal branding after launching Reach in 2001.

As lofty a description as this is, it's still a major injustice. James Naismith is the founder of basketball, but was he a great player by today's standards? In addition to launching his own company, William remains a phenomenal "player," having delivered more personal branding presentations to more people in more places than anyone on earth.

I have no ego issues and quickly saw immense value in learning from William and his curriculum as a means of supplementing my own platform. I quickly added two levels of Reach certification, securing status as both a Reach Personal Branding Strategist and a 360Reach Analyst.

The 360Reach brand survey is a perfect supplement to the SWOT analysis that kicks off the process. It's head and shoulders above any corporate 360 out there in terms of its reliability, accuracy, and focus on reputation as opposed to performance. It ensures anonymity among the people who fill it out for you, which is important because you receive stronger data in the feedback.

Speaking of feedback, let's go back to the case of Sam, our attorney who is looking to become a partner. He's conducted his SWOT analysis with his personal board of directors and has some good information to start with. But Sam is missing some key data points, starting with members of his extended network who care about his personal development: what do they think? It makes sense that his boss, coworkers, friends, family, clients, and others have valuable insight to provide. 360Reach enables you to do this in a fun, quick, and easy way; completing the survey takes only about ten minutes.

Beyond obtaining valuable data for your brand, 360Reach enables you to parse it in a way that lets you compare feedback from different groups from within your network. Often clients will find that there is a disparity between how their brands are perceived among friends, coworkers, and others. This disparity can play a big role in how a broader strategy is formulated.

For example, what if Sam's survey shows that his coworkers are not picking up on one of his core strengths: his strong interpersonal skills. Remember, his board of directors described him as "a person that people gravitate toward." Sometimes discrepancies appear. Perhaps, in his haste to do great work and still get home to his family, Sam confines himself to his office with the door shut and may come across as aloof and unapproachable. This is not an uncommon occurrence, and moving forward, dealing with this should be a focal point of his strategy.

I also like to gauge my clients' sense of self-awareness. In completing the survey, 360Reach makes it a requirement for people to fill out all of the questions on their own before distributing to their network. This accomplishes two things: (1) it gives my clients the opportunity to see what the survey is and understand what their network will be filling out, and (2) it enables them to compare and contrast their own brand perceptions vs. their network's perceptions. Some of the most valuable learning that you can attain about your personal brand is in this process. Understanding your sense of self-awareness is another huge factor in formulating a broader strategy.

A key thing to note here: many people assume that the majority of effort in personal branding goes to addressing weaknesses or developmental areas. The truth is actually the opposite. If you look at good marketing anywhere, the core message is about celebrating and highlighting strengths, not about fixing problems.

The primary goal of strategic planning is to figure out your core strengths—what makes you unique—and bring those qualities to the forefront of your branding efforts. If you discover that there's a developmental need that is prohibiting growth and presents a "threat," that's another story. But the focus, in the immediate future, is to capture your strengths and get them out there in a way that cuts through the ridiculous amount of clutter that faces us every day.

If you're interested in doing a 360Reach brand survey and hiring an analyst to help you, visit www.360reach.me, or feel free to contact me personally, and I can guide you in the right direction. My contact information is at the end of the book.

Armed with a SWOT Analysis and 360Reach survey results, you now have data to guide you strategically. You can answer four key questions that you may not have been able to leading up to the process:

(1)   How is my brand perceived?
(2)   What key strengths do I need to promote?

(3) Do I have weaknesses or threats that need to be addressed?

(4) What immediate and long-term opportunities can I pursue?

At this point in the process, your head is probably overflowing with ideas. Be careful—you can't accomplish everything all at once. I highly recommend making a list of ideas, prioritizing them, and then holding yourself accountable based on realistic deadlines. Get some small victories under your belt and build momentum!

MVB status is now within sight. It's time to give you the tools and tactics to achieve it. The remainder of this book dives into them headfirst.

Chapter 5

● ● ●

Setting a Budget

In addition to comprehensive, well-thought-out strategic plans, successful companies set annual marketing budgets and hold themselves firmly accountable to spend according to pre-established category allocations. Often, a small portion of the budget is left with a nonspecific allocation and labeled "opportunistic," meaning if they come across a new, exciting opportunity to do something that they haven't thought of, they have money to spend on it. And, of course, if revenue or earnings fall below their pro forma annual projections for the year, marketing spending can be "pulled back," with media companies often bearing the brunt of this.

Then, there are everyday people. Only a very small number of them strategically set aside a predetermined amount of money each year to bolster their personal brands. Equally important, very few set aside consistent, regularly scheduled time to work on their brands.

Part of the annual strategic planning process in any personal branding initiative is to create a budget that allocates money and time to growing and cultivating our brands. If you're looking to me for a formula or recommendation for either time or money, I don't have one to offer you. The reason for this is that every case is completely unique. Some of you need a few minutes a day and a minimal cash investment. Others might need to invest significantly more in both areas. These decisions should be made in conjunction with the strategic planning process.

When I formally began working on my personal brand, the initial investment of both time and money was significant. Having worked in marketing in the publishing space for a good chunk of my career, my brand was intrinsically linked to print. Even though I worked with tremendous properties that had many "current" brand extensions (digital, social, etc.), I started to find a subtle stigma attached to a print-related career due to its slow but steady decline in relevance and stature. Unfortunately for me, this fell into the "threat" category of the SWOT analysis. I knew it had to be addressed, and it would require time, money, and thought.

Accordingly, I have allocated dollars in recent years to bolstering my digital capabilities, taking both online and offline courses in Google ad words, analytics, and social media. I then applied as much of my newfound capabilities as I could to my clients, so the investment translated into actual skills and not just certificates for a wall or portfolio. In this way, I have taken specific steps to grow my brand outside of the traditional print realm.

I also devoted many hours to overhauling and bolstering both my social media and overall online presence, so my brand had a contemporary look and feel to it. When someone Google searches my name, I now appear far more often on the first page of a search.

Tactics aside, the key point here is that my efforts are now planned and budgeted annually as part of an overall strategy for my brand's continued growth and development. Like companies,

I set aside a little bit of money in my budget for "opportunistic" spending. If a potentially beneficial opportunity that I didn't anticipate should present itself, I am ready. Also mirroring the corporate model, I reserve the right to pull back money from my budget if my year isn't going well or if there's something outside the scope of work that needs to be addressed.

So what does your budget look like? It might be something as simple as this:

June 2015–June 2016 Personal Branding Budget

Spending

New Headshot	**$400**
Video bio	**$600**
Certification course	**$500**
Networking/entertainment	**$300**
Opportunistic spending	**$300**
TOTAL	**$2,100**

Time

- **Two hours per week on Sundays, 8:00 PM–10:00 PM, devoted to bolstering social presence.**
- **Certification course: 12 total hours, September–October, Wednesdays from 1:00–2:00 PM.**

One final piece of advice: be very wise and judicious with the opportunistic spending allocation. If the perfect opportunity doesn't present itself, don't spend just for the sake of doing so. Trust me when I tell you that most companies hold back on this line item, choosing to apply the money to the bottom line. You can do the same. Or, why not use the savings as an opportunity to do something special: maybe surprise a friend or family member with a gift, dinner, or other special treat.

Speaking of family, I probably don't need to say this, but I highly recommend seeking the approval of any significant other in the budgeting process. I'm confident that you will find them to be extremely helpful and supportive in this process.

Chapter 6

● ● ●

The Lesson of "New Coke" and Authenticity

I remember when I had the first inkling that I might be interested in a career in branding. It goes back thirty years when, as a sixteen-year-old, my favorite drink was Coca-Cola. I was in complete shock with the April 1985 announcement that it would be changing its formula for the first time in almost a century, and it would now be referred to as "New Coke." For the life of me, I couldn't understand why the Coca-Cola Company would do such a thing. I soaked in everything about it—read the newspapers, watched then CEO Roberto Goizueta interviewed on TV—and gradually came to understand the factors that went into the decision: the loss of market share and lethargic growth in the overall soda category. As soon as the new product came out, I rushed to a local deli with my sister, and we each bought a can. I was not a fan, and I switched to Pepsi. Apparently, I was not alone. The public outcry was significant.

Three months later, after the much-heralded and publicly decried launch, "Coke Classic," featuring the original formula, was reintroduced to the market, and the rest is history. The brand soared to new heights and never looked back. I contend that the primary reason that "New Coke" was a failure was that it *lacked authenticity*. It was a blatant attempt to be more like Pepsi. Change was introduced out of fear as opposed to the forward thinking and innovation that was characteristic of the brand.

This case study, though thirty years old, is highly applicable to today's world of personal branding. In short, in any decision-making process, *people gravitate toward authenticity.* This holds true for hiring a business, filling a job opening, establishing strategic partnerships, and so on. When people sense a lack of authenticity, they move in another direction.

There is also no greater source of *protection f*or a personal brand than authenticity. By being true to yourself and consistently staying "on brand," you will attract the right people in all facets of your life and not attract those who are not a fit for you. Unfortunately for me, this is a lesson I learned the hard way. Over time, I've made the mistake of trying to be someone I wasn't and tried to "fit in" in places I didn't belong. The results were not good, and I can promise you, I will do whatever possible to never make that mistake again.

On the flip side, I enjoyed tremendous professional success where I could consistently be my authentic self. For almost a decade, I served as a part of the same five-person senior management team. We each represented different backgrounds, strengths, and opinions. While there were some rocky moments, we worked well together, respected one another, and allowed each other to stay on brand and be our best selves. Each of us was promoted multiple times, and we delivered great results to the company's bottom line. As I look back on it, I'm convinced that much of our success was grounded in authentic leadership.

This book introduces a plethora of strategies and tactics designed to help your personal brand cut through the clutter.

But nothing should be done if it means making a change that takes you away from being true to yourself. The goal here is to do the exact opposite of what Coke did three decades ago when it launched "New Coke." It's to help you *innovate while maintaining authenticity*. This is how MVBs are created!

Furthermore, in any key decision you make in your professional life, always ask yourself, *"Am I staying on brand by doing this,"* before acting on the decision. Always stay true to your authentic self.

Chapter 7

• ● ◉ ◦

LinkedIn:
At the Center of It All

If you're looking for a new job or are open to a new role if approached, check out these statistics published by Career Sherpa in September 2013. The survey detailed executive recruiters' usage of LinkedIn in the hiring process.

- 96% of recruiters use LinkedIn to search for candidates.
- 94% contact candidates directly from LinkedIn.
- 93% keep tabs on potential candidates via LinkedIn.
- 92% vet candidates pre-interview.[1]

Yeah, I would say a good LinkedIn profile is important. Please note: this is just the job search side of the equation. I haven't even touched on networking opportunities or LinkedIn's immense potential in the B2B sales space.

While all components of personal branding play their own important part in the overall growth process, LinkedIn is your designated lead role. I spend a great deal of time with clients, collaborating with them on their profiles. Which leads to the most important point I'm going to make in this book: *if you want to have your personal brand stand out, it's not enough to just play "catch-up." You need to be ahead of the curve.*

How this pertains to LinkedIn is that you need to have a complete profile that aesthetically looks and reads better than others you are competing with. Your profile must motivate people to get in touch with you. In short, *it needs to be the best.* You need to take the extra steps that others aren't willing to, and this means investing time, money, and energy into your profile. Sorry, people, there are no shortcuts here.

Let's get to work! Here are some tips to help you get started:

Have a professional take your headshot

This is your first impression, and you have to make it count. If there's a single place where it makes sense to pay a premium, it's for a photographer that takes a strong headshot. I'm not advising you to spend $1,000 or more, but do your homework, and find someone with an established reputation. A good photographer will advise you on clothing, color, and style. Pose with a relaxed smile, and you'll come across confident and comfortable. As investments go, a good headshot is worth every cent, and you'll be able to use it in many places beyond LinkedIn.

Optimize Your Profile

LinkedIn is like Google in that millions of searches take place there every day, and there is an algorithm that determines how high your profile shows up in any given search. Here are a few immediate things you can do to optimize your profile and improve your brand's ranking in searches:

<u>Complete your profile:</u> You'd be amazed at how many people do not have complete profiles, and this leads to a lower ranking. Think about it from LinkedIn's perspective. It wants to provide users with the best possible experience, and this is simply not going to happen if incomplete profiles come to the forefront of any search. Accordingly, the algorithm rewards those with completed profiles and pushes them higher.

<u>Use the right keywords</u>: LinkedIn is keyword driven. As you write your profile, you have to think about words others will use in a search. Words that might make sense on a resume like "successful," "driven," and "motivated" don't pay dividends here. But if you have your finger on the pulse of what people are looking for, it can make a big difference.

<u>Claim your custom LinkedIn URL</u>: Custom, public-profile URLs are available on a first come, first served basis. For example, I was able to obtain **linkedin.com/in/mikekresch/** because I was the first to claim it. A custom URL helps bolster your rank and offers you further branding opportunities down the road; once you are happy with your profile, you can put it below your signature in e-mails, on your resume, and in other strategic places to drive traffic and further engagement with your brand on LinkedIn.

Here's how to get your custom URL:

1. Move your cursor over *Profile* at the top of your LinkedIn homepage and select *Edit Profile*.
2. Click the URL link under your profile photo. It will be an address such as www.linkedin.com/in/yourname.
3. Under the *Your public profile URL* section on the right, click the Edit icon next to your URL.

4. Type the last part of your new custom URL in the text box.
5. Click **Save**.

<u>Grow your first-degree connections</u>: The more first-degree connections you have, the higher your rank in search. This leads to an interesting debate about whom you invite/accept to be in your network. Some people will argue that just adding connections for the sake of increasing search rank defeats the underlying purpose of LinkedIn as a pure networking vehicle. Others take the opposite approach and are very aggressive in growing their connections, extending invitations to many people that they have never met before.

There's no right or wrong answer here. I might collaborate with two different clients and recommend completely opposite strategies in each case. For example, for a sales director, it might make perfect sense to add as many connections as possible, opening the door to more potential leads. For Sam, our lawyer, I would guide him in the other direction, recommending that he grow his network among people he knows and meets with.

Add Color and Flavor

The strongest profiles on LinkedIn today showcase video, presentations, and assorted visuals that bring life to an otherwise drab screen and provide useful, insightful content that brings a brand to life. Be careful: it's easy to go overboard and completely overwhelm people. A few select vibrant, dynamic options will do the trick. I am a huge proponent of video and recommend this above anything else whenever possible. In chapter 13, I'll discuss this in much more detail.

Develop and Implement a Long-Term LinkedIn Content Strategy

This does not mean that everyone has to go out and create her or his own blog or write a white paper. Even if you're not a strong writer, or simply don't have the time to write an elaborate post, you can still create a strong content strategy for yourself. For example, sharing articles on a consistent basis enables you to stay in touch with your network and provide value. I have a friend in sales who posts inspirational quotes almost every day to his network. This is a very smart content strategy; it consistently reminds his network that he's out there and often produces a smile.

The ultimate win-win scenario is that you create value for your network *and* showcase your expertise at the same time. While this is not always attainable, there is always a strategy available to you that can advance your cause and grow your brand. I'll go into more detail for you about content strategy in Chapter 12.

Be Active with Endorsements and Recommendations

There's no better way to stay in touch with people in your network and remain top of mind than by endorsing them for skills. Want to really get on someone's good side? Send an e-mail and say something such as, *"Hey Jill, hope all is well. I wanted to endorse you for a few skills, but I wasn't sure what was most important to you. What do you suggest?"* In this way, you show Jill that you not only care enough to endorse her but also understand that she has priorities and objectives of her own. It also opens the door to conversation, and you never know where that might lead.

I highly recommend writing authentic recommendations whenever the opportunity arises. In doing so, you provide instant value to someone's profile. Do a strong, heartfelt job with the writing, and your connection will almost certainly post it to her or his profile, leaving a permanent reminder of your good deed, *and* your name becomes a live presence on another profile!

Highlight Your Volunteer Efforts

If a hiring decision comes down to two people, volunteer experience can be a tiebreaker. The reason is that it highlights personal brand attributes that decision makers crave: selflessness, perspective, empathy, and dedication, to name a few. If you have volunteer experience, but it's not on your profile, get it there now! If you haven't done any volunteer work recently, that's OK. There's plenty of opportunity to garner new experiences and help make a difference in the process. I'll go over some great opportunities with you in Chapter 18.

These tips will give you a big head start on the road to LinkedIn success. In the next chapters, we'll explore other facets of social media and how you should be using it to cultivate your personal brand and garner MVB status.

Chapter 8

● ● ● ○

What It Means to Be "Social" Today

Ten years ago, if you gathered a random sample of people from different age groups and backgrounds and asked them to collectively describe a person with strong social skills, my guess is they would have come to at least some level of consensus. The list of traits probably looked something like this:

- Friendly
- Conversational
- Outgoing
- A great host/hostess
- Has a pleasant demeanor
- Genuinely interested in what others have to say
- Looks you in the eye when speaking
- Interacts comfortably with all different types of people
- Entertains others in conversation without being self-absorbed
- Remembers names and faces

- Has a firm handshake
- Stays in touch appropriately

And then, social media entered our lives. It completely muddied the waters on social behavior, adding new layers of complexity. It altered the definition of what it means to be social, and today I argue that you will not be able to generate consensus from that same diverse group of people from a decade ago. Today, if you ask a younger millennial for his description of a person who has strong social skills, he might include protocols for using Instagram and Snapchat. A baby boomer might not have a clue what he's talking about.

The term social media is, in and of itself, a problem. Why? Taken independently, the two words, social and media, are almost a contradiction in terms. We've already discussed what it means to be social. Media consumption, by nature, is antisocial behavior. For example, as a kid, I subscribed to the *Sporting News*. As soon as it arrived at my house, I went into my room, shut the door, and immersed myself in the articles and statistics for two to three hours. Today, my family and I "bond" by watching *Survivor* together on TV. God forbid if anyone should say a word as we watch; she or he will be immediately shushed and told to shut the heck up. Get the picture? Most media consumption, by nature, is not conducive to social activity.

As great as social media is (note: I am a *huge* fan), it has made a complete mess of people's social skills. You have some people, who used to be very social by 2006 standards, who are now constantly glued to their laptops and smart phones, following social media outlets almost to the point of addiction. They can barely hold a conversation without being distracted, missing social cues, turning people off, and completely missing out on opportunities that come with proper social protocol. Many of them still think their social skills are above par, and why wouldn't they? They know all about David and Katie's marriage, have seen great pictures of Tina's Cockapoo, and can describe every hour of James's ski vacation. And more importantly, they are the biggest users of *social* media!

Then there's the contrarian group of people who shy away from social media in spite of its overwhelming influence. They might be incredible at a party, work function, or networking event, but they don't have a complete LinkedIn profile, never post on Facebook, and don't have an active Twitter or Instagram account. They might make a great first impression in person, but it's harder to maintain social relationships today without using basic social media platforms.

One thing hasn't changed in the past decade: *people who have the strongest social skills generate more professional opportunities for themselves and have personal brands that stand out.* Which leads to the million-dollar question: how do you define strong social skills today? I contend that it's an integrated process; let's term it **integrated sociability.** People with strong social skills by today's standards move effectively back and forth between online and offline worlds.

Here's a very simple illustration of integrated sociability in action: you meet a dude named Jeff at a party, have a great conversation, and find that you have a lot in common. You learn that Jeff owns a printing business in a neighboring town. The next day you "friend" him on Facebook, follow him on Instagram, and connect with him on LinkedIn. You don't see or hear from him for a while but have a general idea of what he's up to based on his posts. A few months later, a friend asks you if you know a good local printer. You say that you do, reach out to Jeff, and make an introduction. Jeff gets the business, and you are permanently in his good graces. As an immediate way of saying "Thank you," Jeff goes onto your LinkedIn profile and provides an endorsement.

Here's another example: this one starts online and transitions offline. You are on LinkedIn and see that an old college friend, Laura, pops up as someone LinkedIn suggests that you might know. Upon further examination, you see that she works in a similar industry, and her office is not far from yours. You send her an invitation to connect, along with a personalized message suggesting that meeting for lunch could be a great way to catch up. The lunch conversation is fantastic and opens the door to a viable strategic business partnership for both of you. The business potential would have never materialized were it not for the full, integrated approach. Just connecting on LinkedIn alone would not have led to the immediate opportunity.

Now think about yourself in relation to how you transition back and forth in this world of integrated sociability. Even if you're not doing it effectively now, it's a very easy mindset to adapt moving forward, and you will reap the benefits over time.

Chapter 9

● ◉ ◦ ·

Twitter

After LinkedIn, Twitter is the most important social media property in the world of personal branding. Here are the reasons:

Brand Perception. When you come to someone's Twitter feed, your eye is immediately drawn to the profile images and following numbers. An immediate judgment is made: this person is either a user or a loser. Users garner instant credibility, interest, and following; losers are thrown into the proverbial trash and miss a great opportunity for significant brand engagement.

The Ability to Deliver Value. Like LinkedIn, Twitter makes it very easy to deliver value to a large following. This amplifies your personal brand in a major way and opens the door to many different opportunities.

Education. Twitter is a university unto itself. You can learn an incredible amount of information about topics that are important to you and your career.

Networking. Using Twitter is another great way to meet people, find out about job opportunities, etc.

If you're not yet on Twitter, or stumbled at the gate and gave up a while back, that's OK. There's no better time than the present to build a presence for your brand. To start, I recommend having two Twitter accounts: one that you keep on the "down low" and use to pursue your passions outside of work, and the second should be strictly devoted to work/business.

Let's go back to our attorney Sam for a moment. Let's say that outside of work, he is passionate about professional sports, movies, and do-it-yourself home projects. He should have one account strictly devoted to these interests and use a Twitter handle that masks his name and identity—something like *@CardsFanSam75*. He can follow all the athletes, sports reporters, movie critics, and home improvement gurus he likes but not put any pressure on himself to gain a following. He's *consuming* media here. It's a low-profile activity that, time permitting, he enjoys at his discretion.

His second account should be professional, and here he needs to be *social.* This profile requires great photos for his header and profile and a quality description. I recommend using a simple, easily identifiable handle—something like *@SamJonesNJAttorney.* At a minimum, his short-term goal is to attain 1,000+ quality followers. His long-term goal is to become an influencer, grow and cultivate his following, and most importantly, provide them with value.

Unless you're already a high-profile public figure, you can't simply open an account, tweet a few times, and expect an immediate, organic following. You'll need to get your hands a little dirty at the onset. Here are some tips for the early stages of growing a following:

Look for friends and professional (LinkedIn) contacts that are active. Once you follow them, expect most to quickly follow back. Some might even welcome you with a tweet and encourage their followers to follow you.

Follow relevant companies that show signs of being active and having a high tendency to follow back. You will know this by looking at the number of tweets and the follower-to-following ratio. Even if they don't follow back immediately, there might be a benefit in that their tweets provide subject matter that leads to further engagement, retweeting, etc.

Develop an early tweet/content strategy that engages and provides value to others. This should include a mix of:

- Unique, original posts, using hashtags whenever opportunity and space permit. It always helps if you can find a way to incorporate the hashtag of a trending topic.
- Retweets, featuring positive commentary on the original tweet when possible.
- Content sharing, using bitly.com to shorten links.
- Clicking on "favorite" when you genuinely like someone's tweet.

As always, stay on brand and be authentic with your material.

Follow thought leaders in your industry, and don't be bashful about engaging them in conversation. Once you've grown a following in the 300–400 range, be even more aggressive in following more "everyday" people who have larger followings and show a tendency to follow back. Continue on with a smart, well-thought-out content strategy.

Manage your list of followers. After following someone, wait two weeks to see if they follow protocol and follow you back. If she or he does not, and doesn't offer otherwise useful content, don't hesitate to unfollow. Your goal is to maintain at least an equal ratio of followers to following. It always looks better when the number of people following you is greater than the number of people you are following. But beggars can't be choosers during the early stages of the game.

Leverage Twitter Analytics. See which of your tweets are generating positive responses and engagement, and adapt your strategy accordingly.

Use Lists. As your following grows, you can curate lists of your followers to save time and energy and, in turn, only read tweets from key people. Twitter also enables you to see what lists others have placed you in. This provides added insight into how your content strategy is working and how your followers perceive you.

Avoid politics, religion, and controversy. Save it for a happy hour conversation at a bar. If you simply can't contain yourself, use the other account that you've designated for your hobbies and passions. But don't say you haven't been warned.

Once you pick up some momentum, keep going and growing! You have everything to gain by increasing your brand presence on Twitter. If you really don't enjoy it, you can always slow down after you exceed the magic 1,000-follower number, and use KLOUT (see chapter 11) to maintain your following and presence.

Chapter 10

Facebook and Instagram

Simply put, you cannot afford to be inactive on these properties. Sorry to all of you nonbelievers. It goes back to the concept of integrated sociability and today's definition of being social. Ignoring these forms of social media is antisocial behavior akin to a person who sits alone at a party and refuses to talk to anyone.

Let me illustrate the risk of being inactive with an actual example of a lost opportunity. A few months ago, on a Saturday, I was having lunch with my son at a local diner. A friend whom I hadn't seen for about a year approached us, and it was great to reconnect. After exchanging pleasantries, he commented very warmly on a post of mine that he had enjoyed from a few months prior. Later that day, I checked the post; he hadn't clicked "like."

Do I take that personally? No. Did he make a mistake in not taking a second to click like? You bet he did. In addition to being a friend, this is a person to whom I can refer business. He was not top of mind until we coincidentally bumped into each other, and it probably cost him in his wallet.

MVBs make it a point of keeping their names out there in a positive, self-assured way. Their messaging stays on brand and top of mind. They generate brand awareness and raise their Klout scores. In doing so, they open the door to opportunity.

The beauty of Facebook and Instagram is that they make it easy for you to be active without exerting time and energy. As you embark on the road to integrated sociability, here are ten dos and don'ts to help guide your behavior:

Dos

(1) Do post with the mindset that the CEO of your dream company is reading it. Would she or he approve?

(2) Do make a concerted effort to add friends. It grows your network and social influence, and people always appreciate an invite. In the digital realm, it's almost akin to inviting someone over to your house or apartment.

(3) Do wish people "Happy Birthday." It takes all of three seconds, and it's always appreciated. Best of all, it keeps you at the top of their mind.

(4) Do "like" content that you appreciate, especially from friends who have strategic value.

(5) Do update your profile photo often. It's an easy way to stay active without actually posting anything in words.

(6) Do promote charities and any charitable work that you do without asking for money. For example, you might say, *"Great day volunteering for Habitat for Humanity,"* and post a picture of yourself working on a house.

(7) Do post pictures of kids: sons, daughters, nieces, nephews, cousins, neighbors, etc. Make sure that you ask for permission from parents and guardians.

(8) Do have fun at your own expense.

(9) Do play it safe.

(10) Do remain authentic and always stay on brand.

Don'ts

(1) Don't post between 8 A.M. and 6 P.M. on weekdays. Whatever it is, it can wait a few hours! This also applies to those who use advanced software such as Hootsuite or TweetDeck.

(2) Don't make references to being overworked or being tired because of work, etc.

(3) Don't talk politics and religion. It's worth repeating this point. I know this is a passion for many of you, but here's the reality: politics causes some rational people to behave irrationally, and you don't want to miss an opportunity because someone else is just a little off kilter. Save the heated discussion for drinks over happy hour. And speaking of drinks . . .

(4) Don't show yourself drunk. It sounds obvious, but you'd be surprised how many people make this mistake. It's okay to post an occasional picture of yourself with a drink, but anything more than a few times per year is not recommended.

(5) Don't be mushy. Spare us the kisses, hugs, and cheesy love proclamations. For every person who says, *"Awwww,"* there will be ten who are completely turned off by it.

(6) Don't brag.

(7) Don't showcase affluence or material possessions.

(8) Don't post too often. My rule of thumb is no more than one post a day, two if you absolutely have to.

(9) Don't come across as judgmental.

(10) Don't "unfriend" anyone unless absolutely necessary.

Chapter 11

• • •

Klout

Do you know what Klout is? Do you know your Klout score? Owned by Lithium Technologies, Klout is a website and mobile app founded in 2008. It uses social media analytics to rank its users according to online social influence. Per its website, *"Influence is the ability to drive action. When you share something on social media or in real life, and people respond, that's influence. The more influential you are, the higher your Klout score."*

To get your score, just visit klout.com or download the app. Klout's algorithm quickly generates a score for you between 1 and 100, with 1 being a person with the lowest online social influence, and 99 being Barak Obama, who currently holds the distinction of having more influence than anyone in the US.

The social networks that influence a user's Klout score are Twitter, Facebook, Instagram, Google+, and LinkedIn. Anyone with a Twitter account can register to receive a score. Users who register can then link all of their social networks, and a score is calculated immediately.

Here are some other high-profile names and their scores for you as recorded on 3/1/15:

Lebron James   91
Joe Biden   89
Conan O'Brien   89
Arianna Grande 88
Mark Cuban   87
Robin Roberts   84

The average Klout score is 40. A score of 56 puts you in the top 10 percent, and 63 puts you in the top 5 percent.

In April 2012, *Wired* magazine ran a high-profile article about Klout, detailing the experience of a candidate for a VP-level ad agency job. This candidate was asked for his score in the middle of an interview.[2] He had no clue what Klout was. The interviewer pulled up the screen and had him enter his information. His score was 34. He was later told that he had been eliminated specifically because of his low Klout score.

The article further detailed the potential impact that Klout might have on consumer experiences. It speculated about businesses having access to Klout scores before transactions take place, and the potential implications for those scenarios. With access to Klout data, businesses might consider handling customers with high scores as VIPs in much the same way that celebrities are treated. For example, let's say a hotel knows that a person with a high Klout score is checking in; they might offer something special or assign a better room because of it.

Now take that precedent and apply it across many consumer touch points and businesses. You can see the repercussions: Klout has the potential to make celebrities out of everyday online social influencers. Are we living in a crazy world or what?

Fast-forward three plus years. The good news, or bad news, depending on how you look at it, is that Klout has not become a mainstay in some of the ways that the article projected. Instead, it has switched strategies and become more of a content curator. It has become a very useful site for those of us looking to increase and maintain our Twitter following. Every day it offers users new articles and blog posts in their areas of interest and expertise. Then, with permission, it posts the content to their followings at a scheduled time. It's a smart, highly convenient offer.

What does the future hold for Klout? It's hard to say. A February 2014 article published by Mashable all but stated that Klout had lost some of its clout. To quote author Chris Taylor:

> *"So Klout isn't going away. But it really isn't going anywhere either. You don't hear any clamoring for a Klout IPO—or at least there hasn't been an article hinting at one since 2012. By late 2013, Klout's COO left the company for Uber, the epitome of a startup that most definitely is going somewhere."*[3]

But the fact that it's still around and gaining some traction is great. I love its ability to curate relevant content. More importantly, it provides a tool for tracking and quantifying progress in building online influence. Once you have a Klout score in the mid-50 range, it becomes a marketing tool that you can proactively add to your LinkedIn profile, portfolio, resume, etc.

Chapter 12

● ● ◉ ◦

Content Strategy

Before panic sets in, take a deep breath. That's it. Relax. I'm not going to tell you that starting now you have to publish the next great white paper or that each month you should produce an all-new, 500-word blog post. Nor am I trying to create the next generation of online publishers. If anything, I am sort of a content contrarian.

Let me explain why. Almost two decades ago, when I was really just starting to climb the ladder in the world of media and publishing, I was privy to some fascinating conversations. Early digital executives were grappling with the concept of whether consumers should pay for online content. At that time, traditional media was flourishing; customers were happily paying for magazine subscriptions and for single copies at the newsstand. No one had any issue with paying for cable TV channels. Consumers were more than willing to pay for quality content, and smart business models took advantage of dual revenue models: content and advertising. Inherent logic and precedent to a new business plan called for this approach in any new content-driven business.

And yet, digital executives went the other way. Leading online publishers and up-and-coming content sites opted to give away their content for free and built business models based strictly on ad revenue. Think about the implications had they opted to go the other way and charge for content. Let's take a brand that I worked on for well over a decade, *Popular Mechanics.* Imagine if, in 2000, just as its digital presence started to gain traction, it gave 1 million plus subscribers some great news: they would be able to access all of the incredible past content from the magazine online, plus they would enjoy access to exclusive new articles that would not be found in the magazine. It would only cost them $1 per month—a fraction of the newsstand price.

I have no idea what the conversion rate would have been, but my guess is it probably would have been significant. Had that model and mindset prevailed, the Web as we know it today would be dramatically different. But Wall Street's influence carried the day as analysts placed ridiculously high valuations on media companies based strictly on projections for future ad revenue. Publishers stared at data that indicated they could give away their best content for free and still make millions, and off to the races they went.

Fast-forward to today. Those decisions lay the groundwork for a content world where it is easy to be overwhelmed. The vast majority of digital content is given away for free. And given how easy it is to publish, we are completely overwhelmed with content and often don't have the time to separate the good from the bad. With content marketing being all the rage, don't expect that to change anytime soon.

So while more people are diving into the blog space, I cling to the conviction that good marketing "zigs" when others "zag," and provides a service. Adding to the deluge of blog content because everyone else is doing it isn't necessarily going to differentiate your personal brand in a positive way.

That said, you can still introduce a highly effective online content strategy that bolsters your brand equity. There are many ways to leverage content to add a "halo effect" to your personal brand. Here are some suggestions:

Create a signature, annual, franchise piece of content. Once a year, look to create a single, signature piece of content that your brand owns. Let's term this your Signature Content Offering (SCO). An SCO should showcase a unique aspect of your brand in a fun, engaging way. There are plenty of creative ways to approach this! By formally labeling it as an annual contribution, you apply a level of significance to it, and by restricting it to once a year, you show that you are discerning, and not playing the content deluge game. If you cultivate the platform, you will grow an annual, loyal following of people who look forward to it.

Find a unique, "on brand" way to casually reach out to people. On Monday mornings, I wish both my LinkedIn and Twitter followings a good week. The tactic is "on brand" for me in the spirit of being optimistic and pulling for everyone to advance their careers. It's very brief but keeps my name top of mind without adding clutter.

Talk about job openings as you hear them. Any time you can help someone else find a new job, you are helping both the person doing the search and others who are looking. It's the epitome of a win-win and positions your brand as one that is "in the know" when opportunities arise. If a LinkedIn connection announces that she or he is hiring, you might immediately post something as simple and transparent as this:

"One of my connections, Rich Stanton, is looking to hire a real estate agent and is willing to train. If anyone is interested, let me know, and I will make an introduction."

Build a reputation as a content curator. Prescreen and share quality content with your following. In doing so, you accomplish three things: you provide your network with a valuable service, develop a reputation as someone with a discerning eye, and keep your name top of mind.

In short, there is a world of opportunity to be creative in the content space. You need to approach this with the right mindset and ask yourself the following questions:

- Am I staying on brand?
- Am I doing something unique?
- Am I providing a service?
- Am I effectively staying in touch with my network?

If you can confidently answer "yes" to all four questions, you have yourself a viable content strategy.

● ● ● ●

Chapter 13

Video

I feel confident in predicting that the next big trend in personal branding is video. The proof is in the research. According to a recent blog on Brainshark.com by Sabrina Cote:

- 74% of all Internet traffic in 2017 will be video.
- 65% of video viewers watch more than ¾ of a video.
- Videos in e-mail can boost open rates by 20% and increase click-through rates 2-3x.
- Using the word "video" in e-mail subject lines boosts open rates 19%, reduces unsubscribes by 26%.[4]

Corporate America sees the writing on the wall: video speaks louder than text, drives engagement, and delivers results.

Here's more telling data from Andrew Follet, CEO at Video Brewery:

- 59% of senior executives would rather watch a video than read text.

- 75% of executives told Forbes that they watch work-related videos on websites at least once a week, and 65% of them visit the marketer's website after viewing a video.[5]

There are two primary reasons that most people haven't incorporated video into their personal branding strategy. First, creating a quality amateur video is extremely difficult. Filming is tough, and editing is even tougher. Without experience in the field, the result often looks cheap and unprofessional, which defeats the purpose of the entire initiative. Second, hiring a professional to shoot a video can be expensive, and most people don't even know how to approach a video company to request a quote.

If you're willing to make an investment in the $500–$1,000 range, in a very short period of time, you will have a group of high-quality, edited videos that make your brand really stand out. In addition to being able to communicate your message in a much more efficient way, you will reap the benefits of bolstered SEO and position yourself as a thought leader.

Here is a step-by-step tactical recommendation for approaching the production process:

(1) Find a competent video company with a strong reputation. Check your network and ask friends. I can almost guarantee that you'll have several vendors in a short period of time, which is great, as you can use different quotes for leverage in negotiating price.

(2) When you contact the video companies, say that your goal is to shoot video of yourself for personal branding purposes. You want three videos shot against a green screen. The length of each video will be no more than two minutes. As part of the quote, you can expect two rounds of editing/corrections to be included in the overall cost of

no more than $500. This is a bit low, but you never know; you might draw somebody hungry for the business. Expect to pay a little more than this, but not too much.

(3) The video company might ask you if you want to include "B-roll." This is supplemental footage that is seamlessly edited/mixed into a video. For example, B-roll for Mike Kresch's video bio might include a shot of me pleasantly talking to one of my clients or delivering a speech. It definitely adds to the quality of the viewing experience, but it also adds to the cost. It's your choice if you want to tack this on.

(4) Here are the three videos you want to shoot:
- One that explains who you are and what makes your personal brand unique—your video biography.
- One that offers specific detail about your current role, how you stand out in helping clients, other companies, etc. If you are seeking employment, the concept remains the same: how you will stand out in helping your next employer.
- One that tells a compelling story about you. It can be funny, inspirational, or light-hearted, but it should have content that provides a deeper insight into your personal brand.

(5) Once you've agreed to terms, the videographer will invite you to a given location, most likely her or his studio, for a shoot. Make sure you practice and rehearse your videos multiple times before the day of the shoot. It will probably take one to one-and-a-half hours of set-up time with you there, and then another one to two hours to shoot all three videos. The entire editing process should take about two weeks if done correctly. Don't be bashful about having edits done; you want the final product to be exactly how you want it.

Once you have your videos, here are the next steps:

- Take your video biography and post it under your LinkedIn summary.
- Post the video about your current role under your current job description.
- Create YouTube and Vimeo channels, and post the videos.
- Post all three videos on your personal website if you have one.
- Consider e-mail marketing strategies and outreach for your videos. Remember those earlier statistics about the executives' preference? This is a prime opportunity to tell your story, create networking opportunities, and more!

Videos present an opportunity to be at the forefront of a likely trend. The results are tangible and impactful: your LinkedIn profile stands out, your brand immediately improves its personal SEO (more on that in chapter 14), and you have a tremendous marketing platform at your disposal. The potential return on investment (ROI) is significant. I implore you to go for it!

Chapter 14

• ● ● ●

Personal Search Engine Optimization

I'm sure you've "Googled" your own name before. You're not alone. Thousands of others have already searched for you, and as your personal brand blossoms, expect that number to increase. The key question is: what do the search results look like? My goal, in this chapter, is to give you some quick, simple tactics to improve your rank in search queries and help you dominate the pages.

Let me state from the get-go that I am not a formal SEO expert. I don't know the intricacies and nuances of the Google algorithms, such as Panda and Penguin. Here's the good news: you don't need this level of expertise. The only time I refer clients to SEO experts is if there's a reputation issue that needs to be resolved. In these cases, expect to pay around $500 per month for an ongoing, long-term effort to solve the problem. Over time, the right person can ameliorate the situation. But I warn you, it doesn't happen overnight.

I do have solid, first-hand experience with implementing tactics to bolster personal search ranking. There are multiple people with my name, Mike Kresch, including one seemingly very popular DJ in Pennsylvania. You may have a similar situation. Perhaps you share a name with a professional athlete or celebrity, or maybe your name is common, like Steven Jones or Laura Murphy. People often poke fun at celebrities for coming up with offbeat names for their children. I'll say one thing in their defense: they're making life much easier for their kids in the personal branding realm!

Let's start improving your rank. The good news is, we're already on our way. If you have an optimized LinkedIn profile with a photo and video, then you will soon see that rank higher in a search. The same goes for your Twitter feeds. Don't delete old feeds that continue to show up; change the description and direct people to the newer, more active one that you devote to business. Facebook, YouTube, and Vimeo also rank high in a search.

Here are some added tactics:

Google Plus. It's hard to predict the future of this property. It certainly hasn't caught on the way Google hoped it would. However, given the certainty that Google is indexing it, you should absolutely own and optimize a profile.

Pinterest. This is another fun social media outlet that ranks well in a search.

About.me. This site is a true win-win. It offers bonus exposure and bolsters search rank, and it can drive traffic to social outlets. You can create a free page here in no time—very low-maintenance stuff. For reference, check out my page at about.me/mike.kresch.

Quora. This is a fun site for writing and sharing content, but you don't have to be actively involved to have it bolster your search rank. Simply start a profile, add a bio and picture, and follow a few people and topics. You might even find some great content to share elsewhere.

Personal Websites. Chapter 15 is devoted exclusively to this topic. You'll see a list of websites that can help get you started and some strategic insight as to whether this makes sense for your brand.

Amazon and Barnes & Noble Reviews. If you're a reader and fancy yourself a solid critic, review on these sites for search rank. Be careful though, once you publish, the reviews are permanent. Have passion, avoid typos, and only make a negative comment for a highly compelling reason that won't reflect badly on you.

Chapter 15

● ● ●

Personal Websites

In recent years, we've seen a number of online businesses established to help people create their own personal websites. What's great about these sites is you don't have to hire someone to do any design work or coding. With a little time and energy, you can have a clean, decent-looking site fairly quickly on your own. Well-known players in the personal website space include Weebly, Flavors.me, SquareSpace, and WordPress.

While I will encourage you to pursue this if or when time permits, I don't think creating your own site is a mandatory component of any personal branding strategy. The reason for this is the growing influence of LinkedIn. Anyone looking to research your brand in a business capacity is going to make this a first stop, and an optimized LinkedIn profile is going to rank higher in search than a site you create on any of the aforementioned properties. If you're strapped for time, it's more important to focus your energy on creating a flawless LinkedIn profile.

Here are some scenarios where a personal site can benefit you:

* You enjoy sharing photos of your vacation, hobbies, family, etc., and a personal site presents a fun way to express yourself.
* You're in a highly competitive "battle" for your name in personal SEO, and another opportunity to rank higher is a valuable commodity.
* You're in job search mode and have developed a creative idea for how to use the site to display your portfolio online.
* You're looking to transition your career into a completely different field, and a site like this gives you an opportunity to develop a presence/foundation in another area.
* You're working through an online reputation issue, and a personal site offers an opportunity to showcase another side of you.
* Along the same lines, you see value or opportunity in showcasing more of the personal, "outside-of-work" side of your brand, giving you a more well-rounded online profile.
* You decide to use a site to serve as "home" for a signature content offering (SCO) as discussed in chapter 12. WordPress is probably best suited for this.

I do encourage you to buy the URL for your name if it's available, even if you decide not to create a site. Having control of that URL is important, and you never know what trends may emerge down the road. Whatever you do, approach this area strategically and creatively, and you'll definitely see a benefit in some capacity.

Chapter 16

● ● ●

Online Training

According to the College Board, the average cost of college tuition and fees for 2014–2015 is $31,231 for private schools, $9,139 for in-state public schools, and $22,958 for out-of-state public schools. This does not include room and board, which it estimates at an additional $10,000 minimum, or any personal and transportation expenses.[6]

The big winners here, of course, are the banks, which lend billions of dollars in financial aid and collect interest on loans for years. With tuition costs increasing annually, and many economists projecting a long-term rise in interest rates, many signs point to even heavier student debt over time.

I bring this up because something has to give. And if the situation plays out the way I think it will, a trend will emerge that will have a big impact on personal branding. I'm willing to go out on a limb and make the following statement: unless they adapt to a new world, many renowned colleges and universities may be forced to shut down in the near future. Or at a minimum, to remain competitive, they will need to change the way they charge students. As it stands, a college education is simply too expensive for most Americans, and if these institutions are stubborn enough to maintain the status quo and not adapt in creative ways, then look out!

Here's the beauty of the world today: there are many brilliant people who are not afraid to push the envelope and introduce forward-thinking and innovative solutions to problems. This holds true in the education space. Think about online companies such as Udemy, ALISON, Lynda.com, and Knowledge City, to name a few. Each offers a huge selection of legitimate, highly practical online courses that you can take whenever and wherever you want at significantly lower costs than any university. ALISON's model is particularly intriguing: all courses are 100 percent *free* because the business model relies on ad sales to generate profitability.

Let's take a second to process all of this. Assume that one or more of these businesses gains consistent, high-profile traction in the marketplace by providing a high-quality product that is comparable to a college curriculum. Good, consistent publicity and word of mouth should follow. Further, assume that bold corporate executives from leading companies will eventually publicly state that they are willing to make more concerted efforts to hire students who have certificates from these companies. Why wouldn't they if these students are given a tryout and prove to be valuable in driving results?

I think this is a logical scenario. While it wouldn't result in the demise of the college system as we know it, it should lead to a more level playing field and keep some of our brightest and most talented students out of life-draining debt.

With everything going for them, I predict that at least some of these online education companies will rise in stature, prominence, and reputation, opening up an immediate door to opportunity for all of us to bolster our personal brands. Here are some examples of how we can leverage them:

Career transition. Maybe you're looking to transition your career into a completely different field but don't have the time or money to go back to school. Suppose one of ALISON's sixty free diploma courses is a perfect fit for what you want to do. What's the harm in giving it a test drive? You'll have to work hard to pass (ALISON requires an 80 percent or higher score on tests to attain certification), but you can do it!

Even if you don't find the single perfect course, I'm sure that there are others, possibly even a series of offerings from different sites that will allow you to gradually build your skill set and learn the basics.

Make progress toward a promotion. How many people have found themselves in a situation where a raise or promotion is predicated on learning an advanced skill? The opportunity to obtain these skills is now right in front of us. You can learn on your own time from the comfort of your own home and probably pay much less than you anticipated.

Fill in the gaps. If you're in job search mode, maybe you're getting consistent feedback that there's a gap in your credentials, something specific employers in your target area are looking for, but you don't have—yet. Now, you have places to build your qualifications.

Build your LinkedIn profile. Adding certification(s) not only adds skills, but it also gives you more quality content for your LinkedIn profile. You can add a series of free courses and certifications, and it will look very impressive.

When you have a free moment, take a few minutes to peruse these sites to see if something makes sense for you. Keep your eyes and ears open for developments in this space. It is definitely an area to watch.

Chapter 17

● ● ●

Offline Networking

Even as digital capabilities expand, there is no substitute for face-to-face meetings. Getting out of the office and networking offline is still critical to any personal branding strategy. Personal brands often grow parallel to their network's size and breadth, for logical reasons. Each new meeting grows your network and expands your reach possibilities.

I highly recommend that, each week, you meet at least one new person for networking purposes. You should also schedule at least one networking "maintenance" meeting per week, meaning you choose a person whom you have met before and whom you deem it important to stay in touch with. These meetings are often easier to set up and can be much more "social" by nature, possibly including a meal, happy hour after work, or something along those lines.

Don't even think about telling me that this is too big a time commitment. For argument's sake, let's say you have 112 waking hours during the week. I'm asking you to devote less than 2 percent of that time to meeting with people who can help you grow your brand. If anything, I'm going easy on you.

For some, joining a formal networking group such as Business Network International (BNI), or a Chamber of Commerce is a great way to network. Many people see tremendous ROI from these organizations, and they are proven commodities. If those are not a fit for your personal situation, another way to potentially have face-to-face interaction is to form your own group, perhaps one that caters to your specific industry or line of work.

Even if you decide not to join a group, you should have no trepidation about asking your existing network of contacts to make introductions. You should be proactive in introducing members of your network to one another. This behavior is a staple of everyday business. The golden rule of the game here is always to give first. Let's take me for example. Say there's a human resources executive at a company whom I would love to consult, and for argument's sake, I take a look at his LinkedIn profile, see that it's not optimized, and he doesn't have a strong profile photo. Bingo! If I accomplish nothing else at the first meeting other than helping him out and explaining why it's important to bolster his profile, it's a big win for me.

Sometimes, when a meeting is set up under the label of networking, there's less stress surrounding it. After all, it's not a formal sales call or job interview, and the immediate stakes may be deemed lower. This is a mistake. Always approach a networking opportunity with a sense of urgency, as if the stakes are high. Because they are. You never know what opportunities may present themselves.

Here are some tips as you approach your meeting:

- Have three ideas prepared that specifically focus on how you can help the other person. They should be written down and ready to present on a moment's notice. Your initial focus should always be on giving.

- If possible, save the ideas document onto a flash drive, ideally with your name and/or company name on it, to leave behind. This is a great branding opportunity.
- Avoid mealtime meetings if at all possible. Food is a distraction, and there's always that awkward moment when the check arrives. If this is unavoidable, be aggressive. Pick up the check, tip generously, and chalk it up to a valuable marketing expense.
- You should know early on in the conversation if the relationship has short-term potential for a partnership. If you determine that it does, find the right opportunity to segue cleanly into your ideas and impress the hell out of her or him.
- Be transparent in your closing and overall assessment of the meeting if the future is clear. Examples might be, "We've got a lot of opportunities to follow-up on. Let's talk next steps," or "Even if I can't help you with any of your immediate needs, please don't hesitate to give me a shout if you ever think of anything that I can do."
- In the back of your mind, always think about other people from your network that might find value in an introduction to this person. Even if this specific meeting is not a perfect fit you, it could be a great fit for two others down the road.
- Follow up promptly, and be prepared to execute.
- Don't sweat it if the "giving" leans more on your shoulders at the onset. You're in this to win the marathon, not the sprint, and this meeting is a part of mile one. More often than not, givers cross the finish line first.
- Remember to apply the principle of integrated sociability. As a part of your prompt follow-up, include an invitation to connect on LinkedIn. Follow the person on Twitter if he or she has an active feed. And if the first meeting leads to a second, follow that up with Facebook and Instagram.

Chapter 18

● ◉ ◉ ◦

Creating a Portfolio

Through networking efforts, you've made inroads at a company you'd love to work for. Your dedication and perseverance really start to pay dividends, leading to a networking meeting with Ruby Rogers, a senior vice president at the company, who is in a position to make you a permanent hire if the opportunity presents itself. It will be your first time meeting Ruby in person.

Here are tips for approaching the meeting:

Do your homework. Be prepared, knowing as much as possible about not only the company but also Ruby herself through her LinkedIn profile, Facebook profile, Twitter feed, etc. In fact, if it's possible, a great way to cut the ice is to start off by saying, "I really liked your tweet this morning about X."

Get her talking about things that are high on her priority list. There's no better way to start a meeting off on the right foot than by having Ruby talk about what's important to her right now. In doing so, you can ask questions that showcase your preparation and knowledge of the company. Your goal for later in the meeting is to reference key points she makes and relate them back to your skills and how you can help her.

Cleanly segue into a discussion about you. People are busy, and time is money. You've started the meeting off on the right foot, but Ruby wants to come away with an idea of how you might be able to help her. Don't waste too much time on her agenda. A great way to phrase this is, "I appreciate the information about your company. I know how valuable your time is, so I thought I'd help you learn a little bit more about me, and we can see if there are ways that I can help you even more." She will appreciate this and respect you for managing the flow of the conversation.

Bring out your portfolio for presentation. Ruby is probably expecting you to bring out your resume and walk her through it. But you're about to show her something far more dynamic and engaging: Your brand portfolio!

A portfolio binder is a nicer, slicker-looking version of an old-school loose-leaf binder. If you want a simple, affordable option, I recommend an 8.5" x 11" art portfolio that you can buy on dickblick.com for under $30. This will include pockets that will allow you to showcase up to twenty documents. It gives you an opportunity to tell a much more comprehensive, compelling story and really bring your key accomplishments to life. R emember, the strongest stuff on a resume is usually detailed in one or two lines maximum. Here, you can bring your best stuff to life visually and let Ruby really experience it.

In terms of what to put into your portfolio, this is where marketing and creativity come into play. There are so many different ways to approach this, but here are examples of things you might include:

Work samples. Pick out your strongest stuff!

Awards. You can include the actual certificate or perhaps a picture of you receiving the award.

Certifications. This is an opportunity to showcase your efforts to create a more well-rounded brand for yourself. Because I come from a publishing (paper) background, I include my digital marketing certifications to show proof that I'm well versed in that realm. It's a great opportunity for you to leverage the online sites discussed in chapter 16.

Letter(s) of recommendation. If you don't have anything formal, you can copy and paste recommendations from your LinkedIn profile.

Your social media profile. Now that you've made the effort and bolstered your online presence, show Ruby that your value lies not only in the work that you do but also in your ability to influence others. You can include screen grabs of your Klout score, LinkedIn profile, Twitter feed, etc.

Thought leader content. Let her see your expertise!

Your resume. Note that while it's included, it's only one of many components. In doing this, you take a lot of the emphasis off the resume and make yourself stand out that much more than the typical person Ruby is going to speak to. Including your resume enables Ruby to pass it on if it's needed to facilitate further discussion in any recruiting process. We'll go over some resume tactics in chapter 20.

Other Accomplishments. It's always great to showcase volunteer initiatives, board memberships, and other activities.

Something fun. I include a certification that I have that shows that I completed a successful sky dive. I did a jump over a decade ago with clients, and I use it to showcase that I am a true team player who is willing to try any and all new things in the spirit of advancing the cause. Here you might include pictures of your family, or maybe a picture of yourself engaged in a hobby.

A strong, customized closing statement. Summarize your brand succinctly, and explain the synergy with Ruby's company.

How do you leave all of this great information with Ruby? The easiest way is to take all of the documents and put them on a flash drive for her future reference. And if she ever needs your resume, it's easy for her to find. In doing this, you're also leaving her with a nice gift with some value, and it saves paper.

As noted in chapter 17, if you have the budget, an even stronger way to accomplish this is by putting them on a branded flash drive with your name on it. Not only is this impressive, but also there is a real possibility that your name will sit on her desk for a long time after the meeting.

Chapter 19

● ◦ ◦ ◦

The Death of the Resume

I'm not exactly going out on a limb when I say that resumes will probably be extinct within a few years. If you don't buy into this statement, please answer these questions for me:

- *What value does a resume offer a recruiter that LinkedIn doesn't?*
- *Can you proactively search for a resume online?*
- *Does a resume allow you to showcase projects, video, endorsements or references?*

It's an outdated product, plain and simple. Combine that with the numbers we looked at with recruiters' LinkedIn usage, and you can see the direction of where things are going. That said, it remains a part of today's recruitment process, so let's add building a solid resume to the mix of tactics that we use to cultivate your personal brand.

I'm going to start out by giving you some safe, tried and true suggestions that have "held court" in resume building for many decades. But I'm not doing my job if I don't at least give you suggestions for cutting through the massive clutter. So I will offer you three "out-of-the-box" ideas in addition to this, which you should absolutely consider if you are in active job-search mode.

THE "SAFE STUFF"

Consider hiring a professional resume writer. There are many very talented people out there who do this. It may cost you a good chunk of your budget, but it does take one giant task off your plate. Assuming you hire the right person, you have the security of knowing that the content is both strong and grammatically correct.

Have a proofreader check grammar and punctuation. This is significantly less expensive than a writer, and it maintains the authenticity of the content, meaning they're your words as opposed to someone else's. Nine times out of ten, I recommend that you go this route if possible.

Quantify your accomplishments as much as possible. Everyone writes that they exceeded goals, brought in new accounts, and so on. Save the recruiter the time and energy of asking the inevitable question and provide more quantitative detail. How much revenue were you responsible for bringing in or saving? How much did your actions directly impact the bottom line?

Be authentic. Any strong, experienced recruiter will be able to quickly see whether a resume is filled with authentic substance or a lot of fluff. Keep it real. Don't stress the fact that you don't have the perfect resume. No one does!

Limit the length to two pages. If you have to trim, get rid of older stuff that you can't quantify.

THE "MIKE EARNS HIS PAYCHECK" STUFF

Here are tactics that you may not see or hear elsewhere that are designed to help you stand out without crossing the line when it comes to proper protocol.

The Pink Car Theory. Imagine that you're driving from point A to point B on the highway. In doing so, you pass hundreds of cars: new, old, very expensive, cheap, etc. One of the cars happens to be painted bright pink. At the end of the day, which car do you remember? The pink one! It's the way our brains function.

My point is that if you're in a situation where you don't have an "in" on a job and are blindly submitting your resume, you have about a one in one thousand chance of being considered, let alone being called in for an interview. In these instances, you have to take a chance. Put your resume on colored paper that will unquestionably stand out.

Add a social media profile to your resume. If I ask you, "Which is more important, your educational background or current social media profile?" What would your response be? For me, I put roughly equal weight on both, with maybe a slight edge to social media because it's more relevant to my immediate situation.

The mere fact that this is a debatable topic showcases an inherent flaw with current resume formats. Everyone includes her or his education, but no one includes a social media profile. That is, except my clients! Here is a format that I recommend to be positioned either before or after your education:

SOCIAL MEDIA PROFILE

<u>Klout Score</u>: 56 (top 10%)

<u>LinkedIn</u>: 930 connections, 25 Groups, "all-star" profile. Publish monthly articles, averaging 250 reads, 12 "thumbs up" reviews.

<u>Twitter</u>: 1,275 followers. Used to stay up-to-date on industry trends and actively engage in professional dialogue with other attorneys.

<u>Facebook</u>: 820 friends. Moderately active to share photos of family and stay in touch with friends.

<u>Instagram</u>: 330 followers. Periodically upload family photos.

<u>Google+</u>: Updated profile but not active.

Replace your professional summary at the top with a colorful chart. As the saying goes, you have one chance to make a first impression. A great opportunity to do this, while really standing out, is to replace the professional summary at the top of your resume, which everyone has, and replace it with a colorful graphic that accomplishes the same thing. Here are two examples:

(1)   A pie graph that breaks down all the components of your experience by percentage.

(2)   A bar graph that shows revenue or savings increases that you personally are responsible for in your current role.

Not only will this make your resume "pop," it almost guarantees where the first question will come from, and you can be fully prepared with a well-scripted answer.

Chapter 20

● ● ● ●

Volunteer!

"It's easy to make a buck.
It's a lot tougher to make a difference."
—*Tom Brokaw*[7]

I don't completely agree with Brokaw; it's not necessarily easy to make a buck these days. I do, however, concur that it's a lot tougher to make a difference. Unfortunately, the nine-to-five workday is a distant memory for many of us. We work longer and harder, busting our butts to get things done as quickly and effectively as we can, and then rush off to attend to family and other outside obligations. This doesn't leave us with much time for *ourselves*, let alone for making a difference in the lives of others.

It's significantly tougher for today's professional to make a difference in the lives of others through volunteering. Those who do manage to volunteer are held in very high regard; as noted in chapter 7, strong volunteer experience speaks volumes about someone's ability to go the extra mile and immediately associates her or him with attributes such as selflessness, perspective, empathy, and dedication. It's like adding an extra layer of polish to a personal brand, and the shine resonates brightly.

My recommendation to everyone is to *find the time to volunteer.* I know how hard it is, but make it happen. If you do it right, it will pay huge, life-changing dividends, open up doors to new people and opportunities, and most importantly, provide an increased sense of personal satisfaction, pride, and self-worth. The world needs a lot of help, and although we are pressed for time, we have a lot of potential to give back.

The best way to approach this is not to just go out and volunteer for the first opportunity that presents itself. Take the time to find something that you believe strongly in and enjoy doing; with this approach, the likelihood of it becoming a fixture in your life is greater.

If you need help getting started, here are some websites that help match volunteers with causes:

www.volunteermatch.org
www.idealist.org
www.allforgood.org

Here are some other specific thoughts and ideas pertaining to volunteer opportunities:

Animals. Anyone who is passionate about animals should know that local shelters are often in need of help. If you want to get a listing of shelters near you, www.petfinder.com has a tool that will locate them.

Big Brothers/Big Sisters. I did this myself for over four years. There's no bigger way to make an impact on a child's life than through this program. Visit www.bbbs.org.

Physical Fitness Events. For those of you who love to work out, what better way to leverage your passion than by training for and participating in cause-related activities, such as walkathon's, runs, etc.?

Scholarship Fund. As the cost of a college education continues to skyrocket, the need for scholarships is increasing that much more. Starting your own scholarship is an incredible way to make a difference. For more information, visit www.ScholarshipExperts.com.

Hospital volunteers. Simply go to the Web, research local hospitals, find the name of the local volunteer coordinator, and reach out!

Fresh Air Fund. If you live in a rural setting, the Fresh Air Fund is a great way for you to provide an inner-city child the gift of spending a summer away from the trouble and heat of the city streets. Learn more at www.freshair.org.

Your local house of worship. There are many volunteer opportunities to be found there.

Habitat for Humanity, Rebuilding Together. If you like do-it-yourself projects, painting, etc., there is no better volunteer opportunity than working with these organizations. You can form a group of your own or ask to be included in an ongoing project. For more information, visit:

www.habitat.org
www.rebuildingtogether.org

College/University Alumni Clubs. I recently signed on to help support my regional alumni chapter of Columbia University, where I attended business school. I look at it as an opportunity to give back for the incredible education I received. Alumni groups often need a lot of help with events, membership, and interviews; if you're interested, it won't be too hard to get involved.

As important as it is to volunteer, it's equally important to share the experience itself with your network. I am a huge proponent of being vocal and outgoing in support of volunteering. This accomplishes two things. First and foremost, it lends support to the cause. You never know who you might recruit to help you, and the opportunities that the subsequent interaction could lead to. And, of course, it markets your participation. Don't assume that people will just remember the line item on your LinkedIn profile. As admirable and rewarding as it is to volunteer, you should be recognized for making the effort and caring.

Chapter 21

• ● ● ●

Brainstorming

My creativity is at its acme when I'm taking my morning shower or on a Precor machine at the gym. I'm sure many of you can also identify those points in time where your brain feels "in the mood" to feed you ideas. Whenever these ideas come to you, make sure you find a place to record them or write them down quickly, so you don't forget. I keep a pad and pen in the bathroom so when that AM idea hits me, I don't lose it. I also recommend brainstorming with a group as a means of generating ideas for your future.

Here's how to approach this: once a year, you organize a small group of people to get together and brainstorm each other's brands, careers, etc. It might be an opportunity to bring back your board of directors from the SWOT analysis. Or, maybe it's an entirely new group of people; it's up to you. As long as it's a team of smart, well-intentioned people who are willing to put their egos aside and dive head first into tackling a challenge, you're in a good place.

As you can probably tell by now, I tend to err on the conservative side of things. But at these sessions, I encourage everyone to let it all out. Be innovative. Challenge the group to think as creatively as they can. No idea is too far-fetched. Everyone's goal from this session is to *implement one idea*, something new and fresh, an idea that had never crossed your mind before. Then, repeat the process on an annual basis. It should be a fun session; I see no harm in doing this over dinner or drinks.

By pushing the creative envelope, I'm not suggesting that you go out on a limb and do something irresponsible. I'm not looking for you to drop the successful, high-powered career to open a restaurant on a beach in Costa Rica. My point here is that companies that come up with such wonderful, creative, "never-been-done" ideas often come up with them by putting together cross-functional teams to brainstorm. There's no reason this process can't be applied to personal brands.

Chapter 22

● ● ◉ ◦

Let's Do This!

Remember back in chapter 1, we identified the ten characteristics observed in MVB winners? Let's revisit them and now add a reference to the chapter(s) in the book that can help you craft each trait:

(1) They have a growth strategy for their brand in place. Chapters 3–5 review some good starting points for developing a formal strategy for your brand.

(2) They are authentic and always stay "on brand." In chapter 6, we revisit the story of "New Coke," which is a nice illustration in support of this concept. No matter how the world evolves, authenticity will always remain an integral component of personal branding and a key to your happiness as well!

(3) They are happy at work. Speaking of happiness, I sincerely hope you are already in a good place professionally. If not, start diving into the tactics presented throughout this book,

and put yourself in a position to get to exactly where you want to be. You deserve it.

(4) They rank well in a search. Chapter 7 and chapter 14 provide immediate tips and tactics to help with rank.

(5) They have a strong social media presence. Chapters 7–11 cover this in detail. Remember to register for Klout and start monitoring your improvement. In addition to being a source of pride, your Klout score can turn into an immediate marketing vehicle, particularly for your portfolio (chapter 19) and resume (chapter 20).

(6) They learn new skills. Chapter 16 offers some valuable, affordable options in the online certification space. Beyond these sites, there are countless resources available to you. Pick up a new skill and start applying it.

(7) They have a valuable, growing network of contacts, followers, and friends. Pay particular attention to chapter 8 and the concept of integrated sociability. Chapter 12 gets you started on formulating a content strategy to keep your network engaged in growth mode. Chapter 17 also gives you some sound advice for effective offline networking.

(8) They give back. Chapter 18 provides a menu of suggestions for being an active volunteer. There are an infinite number of ways to give back, so find a cause that you are passionate about and ask how you can help.

(9) They try new things without trepidation. Many of the concepts throughout this book will be new to you. Try them

out. Conduct an annual brainstorming session, as described in Chapter 21, and implement one new idea that comes out of it!

(10) They are prepared for anything. I have no doubt that if you apply the insight, strategy, and tactics that this book presents, you will be prepared to seize any opportunity that comes your way and be well equipped to handle the inevitable setbacks that rear their ugly heads from time to time.

And with that, I wish you nothing but the best of luck in attaining MVB status. When you reach it, you will find yourself on top of the world, greeted by an open door filled with opportunity!

Please stay in touch, and let me know how you are doing. I am always open to feedback, too. You can reach me on Twitter @MikeKresch, or via e-mail at mike@kreschandpartners.com. I promise to write back!

References

1   Hannah Morgan, *"The ROI of Social Recruiting Exists,"* September 11, 2013, Careersherpa.net/the-roi-of-social-recruiting-exists/
2   Seth Stevenson, *"What Your Klout Score Really Means,"* April 24, 2012, Wired.com/2012/04/ff.klout/
3   Chris Taylor, *"Why Klout Had to Change,"* February 10, 2014, Mashable.com/2014/02/10/-why-klout-had-to-change
4   Sabrina Cote, *"10 Powerful Video Statistics (and What They Mean to You),"* March 11,2014, brainshark.com/Ideas-Blog/2014/March/ten-video-marketing-statistics-and-what-they-mean-to-you.aspx
5   Andrew Follet, 18 Big Video Marketing Statistics and What They Mean for Your Business, No date listed, www.videobrewery.com/blog/18-video-marketing-statistics
6   Collegedata.com, What's the Price Tag for a College Education?, www.collegedata.com/cs/content/content_payarticle_tmpl.jhtml?articleID=10064
7   BrainyQuote.com

www.ingramcontent.com/pod-product-compliance
Lightning Source LLC
Chambersburg PA
CBHW071243170526
45165CB00003B/1220